Food
APPLES

Louise Spilsbury

Heinemann
LIBRARY

www.heinemann.co.uk/library
Visit our website to find out more information about Heinemann Library books.

To order:
 Phone 44 (0) 1865 888066
 Send a fax to 44 (0) 1865 314091
 Visit the Heinemann Bookshop at www.heinemann.co.uk/library to browse our catalogue and order online.

First published in Great Britain by Heinemann Library,
Halley Court, Jordan Hill, Oxford OX2 8EJ
a division of Reed Educational and Professional Publishing Ltd.
Heinemann is a registered trademark of Reed Educational & Professional Publishing Ltd.

OXFORD MELBOURNE AUCKLAND
JOHANNESBURG BLANTYRE GABORONE
IBADAN PORTSMOUTH (NH) USA CHICAGO

© Reed Educational and Professional Publishing Ltd 2001
The moral right of the proprietor has been asserted.

Designed by Celia Floyd
Illustrated by Tokay Interactive
Originated by Ambassador Litho Ltd
Printed by South China Printing Co in Hong Kong.

ISBN 0 431 12708 5 (hardback)
05 04 03 02 01
10 9 8 7 6 5 4 3 2 1

British Library Cataloguing in Publication Data
Spilsbury, Louise
   Apples. – (Food)
   1. Apples 2. Cookery (Apples)
   I. Title
   641.3'411

Acknowledgements
The Publishers would like to thank the following for permission to reproduce photographs:
Amazone p.16; Corbis pp.8, 12, /Ed Young p.20, /Paul Seheult p.21, /Michael S Yamashita pp.18, 19; Gareth Boden pp.6, 7, 22, 23, 25, 28, 29; Image Bank p.24; Oxford Scientific Films/Mike Slater p.17; Peter Newark's American Pictures p.9; PhotoDisc pp.14, /J Luke; Roger Scruton p.15, /Photoshop p.13; Tony Stone /James Darell p.4, /Jake Rais p.5, /Andy Sacks p.11.

Cover photograph reproduced with permission of Gareth Boden.

Every effort has been made to contact copyright holders of any material reproduced in this book. Any omissions will be rectified in subsequent printings if notice is given to the Publisher.

CONTENTS

Words written in bold, **like this**, are explained in the Glossary.

WHAT ARE APPLES?

Apples are a kind of **fruit** that we can eat. People eat more apples than any other fruit in the world.

Apples grow on trees. Most of the apples we eat are grown in **orchards**. Orchards are pieces of land where many fruit trees grow.

KINDS OF APPLES

There are thousands of different kinds of apples. You can divide them into two main kinds – dessert and cooking apples. Dessert apples taste sweet and you can eat them **raw**.

Cooking apples are hard. They taste **sour** if you eat them raw. You need to cook them before you can eat them.

IN THE PAST

The **Romans** grew apple trees so they could eat the **fruit**. They planted **orchards** in England. This Roman **mosaic** shows a bird on an apple.

English people took apple **seeds** to America 300 years ago. Later, a famous man, known as 'Johnny Appleseed', travelled all over America, giving away and planting apple seeds.

AROUND THE WORLD

This map shows some of the countries that grow the most apples. Apples grow best in countries that have warm summers and chilly winters.

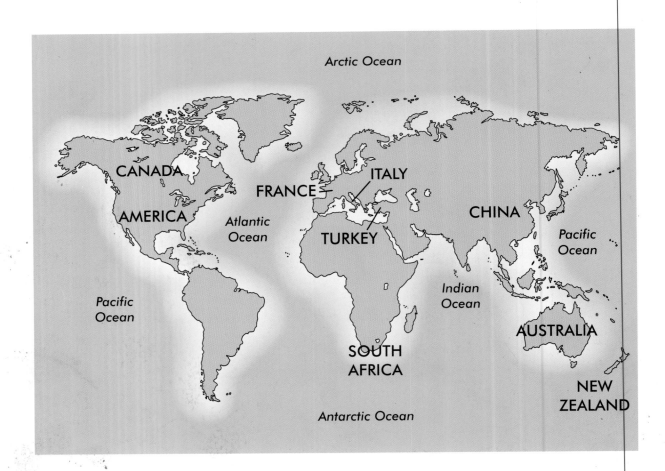

America is the world's biggest apple **producer**. This means it grows more apples than any other country. Ships from America carry apples to other countries. This is called **exporting**.

LOOKING AT APPLES

Like all plants, apple trees need water, **nutrients** and sunlight to grow. Roots take in water and nutrients from the soil. The branches hold up the leaves to reach light.

leaves

branch

trunk

roots
(these are
mostly
underground)

Inside an apple, the **core** holds the **seeds**. The stalk is the part that attached the apple to the tree. We can eat the flesh and the **peel**.

stalk   peel   flesh   seeds

core

APPLE TREES

In spring apple trees grow flowers. Bees come to the **orchard** to visit the flowers. When the bees drink **nectar** from the flowers, yellow **pollen** clings to their bodies.

When the bees land on different trees, the pollen rubs off onto their flowers. The pollen makes new **seeds** grow in these flowers. The apple **fruit** begins to grow around these seeds.

15

GROWING APPLES

The apples grow in summer. Some farmers feed the trees with **fertilizers**. Fertilizers help the trees grow big, juicy apples.

Many farmers also spray the trees with **pesticides**. These sprays stop insects from eating and spoiling the apples.

17

PICKING APPLES

In autumn the apples are ready to eat. Most apples are picked by hand because they **bruise** easily. Farmers keep apple trees short so the apples are easy to reach.

The apples are washed in big machines. Then farmers store the apples in very cold rooms. This keeps them fresh until the farmers sell them.

APPLES TO BUY

Before going to **consumers**, apples are sorted by hand. Damaged ones are thrown away. Then the good apples are sorted into different sizes by a machine.

The apples are packed into smaller boxes. In between the layers is soft paper. This stops the apples knocking against each other.

EATING APPLES

Most apples are eaten **raw**, on their own or in fruit salads. Other apples are used for cooking sweet and **savoury** dishes. Apple sauce goes with many dishes.

Apples are also **processed** in different ways. They may be used in jam with other fruits, as fruit pie fillings, or in jellies. Apples are also used to make fruit juices.

GOOD FOR YOU

Apples contain **nutrients** that give us energy and keep us healthy. They also contain **vitamins** that help our bodies to grow and protect us from illness.

Do you eat apple **peel**? It is good for you. Apple peel contains **fibre**. As fibre passes through your body, it keeps your **digestive system** clean and healthy.

Wash the apple first, if you want to eat its peel.

HEALTHY EATING

This food pyramid shows the different foods you need to eat to stay healthy.

Most of the foods you eat each day should come from the base of the pyramid.

The top of the pyramid shows the foods you should eat the least of. Apples belong in the middle of the pyramid. Eat more of the foods from the middle section than from the top.

The foods shown in each part of the pyramid help your body in different ways.

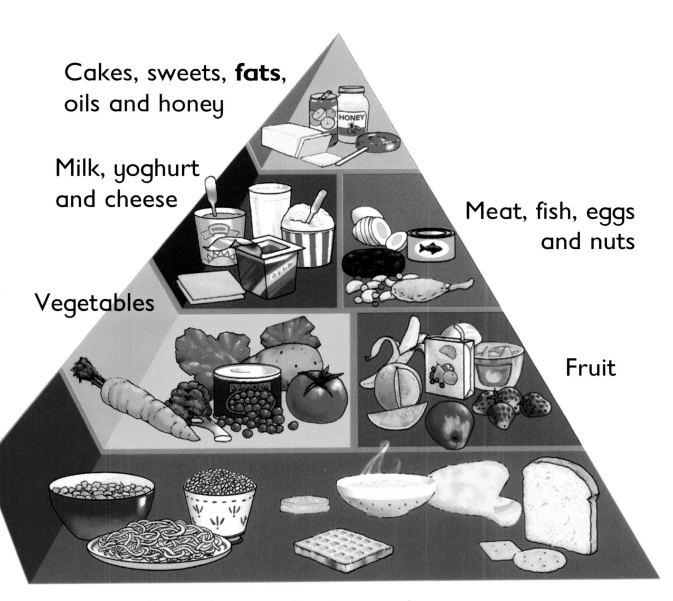

Cakes, sweets, **fats**, oils and honey

Milk, yoghurt and cheese

Meat, fish, eggs and nuts

Vegetables

Fruit

Bread, cereals, rice and pasta

APPLE SAUCE RECIPE

1 Cut the **peel** off the apples and chop them into pieces.

2 Put the pieces into a pan and cover with water.

3 Cook gently until the apple is soft.

You will need:
- 2 large apples
- water
- spoonful of honey
- pinch of cinnamon

Ask an adult to help you!

4 Pour the cooked apple into an electric blender.

5 Blend until you have made a smooth sauce. Add the honey, and a little cinnamon if you like.

6 Serve the sauce warm or cold.

GLOSSARY

bruise mark caused when fruit is knocked. The part that is damaged then goes bad.

consumers people who buy things they need or want, like food

core inside a fruit like an apple, the core holds and protects the seeds

digestive system parts of your body that break down food into tiny bits. Your body turns the digested food into energy to keep you well and help you grow.

exporting when food or other goods are taken from one country to be sold in another

fat type of food. Butter, oil and margarine are kinds of fat.

fertilizers sprays or powders that help plants grow bigger and produce more fruit

fibre parts of a plant that our bodies cannot completely digest

fruit part of a plant that grows around the seeds to protect them

mosaic small pieces of stone or pottery put together to make a picture

nectar sweet juice in the centre of a flower

30

nutrients food that gives plants and animals the goodness they need to grow and stay healthy

orchards pieces of land where apple trees are grown in rows

peel 'skin' of an apple

pesticides sprays farmers use to kill insects and other creatures that damage their crops

pollen tiny yellow specks on a flower. Pollen helps to make seeds that grow into new plants.

processed when food is cooked or treated in a certain way to make a new kind of food or drink. Apples are processed to make apple juice.

producers people or countries who make or grow food or goods to sell

raw not cooked

Romans Romans ruled over many lands, including Britain and much of the rest of Europe for about 800 years (from 510 BC to AD 410)

savoury not sweet

seed part of a plant that can grow into a new plant

sour bitter. Lemons and vinegar taste sour.

vitamins nutrients in some foods that help us grow and protect our bodies from illness

MORE BOOKS TO READ

Life Cycle of an Apple, Angela Royston, Heinemann Library, 1998

Safe and Sound: Eat Well, Angela Royston, Heinemann Library, 1999

Plants: Flowers, Fruits and Seeds, Angela Royston, Heinemann Library, 1999

Senses: Tasting, Karen Hartley, Chris Macro, Phillip Taylor, Heinemann Library, 2000

The Senses: Taste, Hodder Wayland

INDEX

Titles in the *Food* series include:

Hardback   0 431 12708 5

Hardback   0 431 12700 X

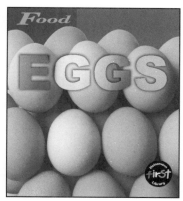

Hardback   0 431 12702 6

Hardback   0 431 12706 9

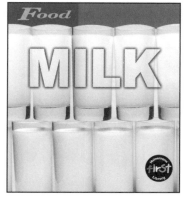

Hardback   0 431 12701 8

Hardback   0 431 12703 4

Hardback   0 431 12707 7

Hardback   0 431 12705 0

Find out about the other titles in this series on our website www.heinemann.co.uk/library